MW00440916

Teaching the World to Die

Unitarian Universalist Attitudes

Regarding Death

AN ESSAY OF HISTORY AND OPINION

Edward Searl

TEACHING THE WORLD TO DIE by Edward Searl

ISBN: 9781983131691

Copyright © 2018 by Edward Searl
The Royal Nonesuch Press
Chadds Ford, PA

TEACHING THE WORLD TO DIE

UNITARIAN UNIVERSALIST ATTITUDES REGARDING DEATH

Love is a flame; -- we have beaconed the world's night.
A city: -- and we have built it, these and I.
An emperor: -- we have taught the world to die.

from "The Great Lover," Rupert Brooke

MT. AUBURN AND THE RURAL CEMETERY REFORM

Unitarians contributed mightily to what the historian and literary critic Van Wyck Brooks aptly described (1936) as "The Flowering of New England." The years 1815 through 1865 were yeasty decades as the emergent American Republic sought an identity distinct from European antecedents, while applying the heady Enlightenment values embodied in the Constitution. Unitarian minister Theodore Parker—of the place and era—spoke of a nation "of all the people, by all the people, for all the people." Destiny seemingly charged the American people to make the world anew. Boston was the Athens of America. And the newly minted liberal religion called Unitarianism defined Boston culture.

Particularly among the Unitarians, optimism in regards to the human condition and society prevailed. There was a pervasive sense that society, as well as self, were young, malleable, and forward looking. Reform movements and voluntary associations flourished, bringing important changes from what we now describe as "the bottom up."

Among the reform movements of the antebellum era, concerns about the disposal of the dead resulted in a cultural phenomenon known as the rural (garden) cemetery movement. Unitarians led the way in creating the young nation's first "rural cemetery." (*Cemetery* in the classical Greek sense literally means "place of repose.")

Mt. Auburn Cemetery, some five miles outside of Boston, dedicated in 1831, set a high standard, compelling interest and imitation for exurban, landscaped burial grounds. Picturesque Mt. Auburn was an immediate tourist destination, perhaps equal to the sublime Niagara Falls, long America's major attraction. Throughout the antebellum era, thousands of the curious made a pilgrimage to see this much talked about innovation in deathways.

Mt. Auburn inspired scores of similar "places of repose," where the dead were interred or entombed and the living visited to remember and reflect. The setting, seventy-two original acres of rolling land with the entrance in Cambridge and most of the property in Watertown, already was hallowed for the spirit of place—what the ancient Greeks called *genius loci*. Harvard students, including Emerson, who had roamed the overgrown, old Simon Stone farm, had nicknamed it "Sweet Auburn," after an Oliver Goldsmith poem "the Deserted Village." The landscape and a decaying building suited the aesthetic of the picturesque. (Since much of the original growth remained, Mt. Auburn was a *rural* cemetery. Many of the imitators were more properly *garden* cemeteries, landscaped from cleared ground.)

The picturesque was one of several trends of the day that converged in the making of Mt. Auburn Cemetery. The most significant factor involved the growth of cities, Boston in particular, and the condition of the city's existing graveyards.

By the early 1800s, city graveyards had become overcrowded, untended, and unsanitary. Physicians and scientists proposed that urban burying grounds released putrid and unhealthy "miasma."

In 1823 Boston, a burial controversy erupted, instigated by the 1819 erection of a new and expensive Episcopal church, St. Paul's. Unitarians, republican heirs of Puritanism, worried that this might be an attempt to restore Toryism and High Church practices in particular. They objected to forty-seven family crypts proposed for the new church's basement, setting off what became known as the "burial controversy." The controversy resulted not only in rejection of the proposed crypts but also in the closing of most of the old Boston graveyards to new burials. Unitarian Josiah Quincy, known as city's Great Mayor, led the debate and leaned toward the reformation of burial practices, thereby begging new arrangements outside the city. As a result, death was soon to be taken out of burgeoning Boston, into the country, where Nature would cast death in new sensibilities.

Two years after the burial controversy, the Unitarian editor of the *New-England Galaxy*, Joseph Buckingham, wrote: 'Who would wish to be buried in a close city and a crowded graveyard to be deranged and knocked about, separated and disjointed long before the last trumpet sounds. Would we not rather lie serenely where the pure breeze rustles the honeysuckles, and the field flowers, the long grass and the drooping willow, which hover and hang over our grasses. Where, secure from unhallowed footsteps and boisterous mirth, the reeling tread of the drunkard, or the vapid gaze of the thoughtless, we lie quiet, undisturbed and happy?"

The New England Transcendentalist worldview, marking the transition from a first to a second generation of Unitarians, was coincident with larger trends, as Romanticism layered the Enlightenment ways of the founders. Nature played prominently among the Transcendentalist Unitarians, often labeled as pantheists because of their love for Nature. The Unitarian poet William Cullen Bryant's 1819 influential poem on death, "Thanatopsis,'' was as much a poem about Nature as it was a meditation on death. However, what became Mt. Auburn Cemetery was not merely a natural setting, but a natural setting sculpted by an aesthetic known as the *picturesque*.

The picturesque is properly seen in context of earlier popular aesthetics: the beautiful and the sublime. The former involves sensibilities that are pleasing, in which one reposes in beauty with satisfaction. An undisturbed pastoral scene has beguiling beauty. In contrast, the sublime has in it aspects of awe and even fear. Niagara Falls, powerful, dangerous, and compelling, epitomized the sublime. The picturesque has in it a sense of time and possibly decay, along with a natural beauty. The result is a sensibility of bittersweet melancholy, evoking an awareness of the transiency of Life and leading to melancholic reflections on human mortality. The picturesque incorporated aspects of both the beautiful and the sublime.

In the 18th century, the picturesque took form in English Gardens intended to evoke moral sentiments by combining naturalistic elements (such as the weeping willow) with curving paths and walkways, grottoes and caves, as well as monuments and statuary. Monuments suited a newfound desire of the American Republic to venerate and commemorate founders and forebears, while uplifting the significance of the new nation. (A monument to the Battle of Bunker Hill proposed in 1823 rose from a need to commemorate heroes and events of the Revolution. It resulted in an impressive 220-foot tall obelisk completed in 1843.)

In this culture of optimistic ferment, the commemoration of the individual coincided with an emerging Unitarian optimistic estimation of the human condition. The leading Unitarian minister of the first generation, William Ellery

Channing, made it clear that humankind could seek a "likeness to God," through reason and free will. A second generation of Unitarian Transcendentalists led by Emerson further extolled the goodness and abilities of each ingenuous person. ("Trust thyself.") The Puritans from whom the Unitarians emerged, of course, viewed the human condition pessimistically, hence simple slabs or no slabs at all marked their graves.

The value of the person found deeper resonance in a sentiment for family. The family plots at Mt. Auburn served to venerate ancestors, as well as to institutionalize (and set boundaries on) grief in an era marked by death, particularly of children. Melancholy, a sweet grief, infused a century distinguished by what was later characterized as a culture of death.

Two other Unitarian attitudes played on the founding of Mt. Auburn. Voluntarism, the notion that committed individuals rather than the state should take responsibility for reform and philanthropy, resulted in the selling of Mt. Auburn lots to the general public. Privately funded, it was available to all who wished to subscribe. It was essentially a public institution. The core attitude of Unitarian tolerance, the aim to rise above sectarianism prevailed from the beginning. Though spiritual in its intentions, America's first rural cemetery bent toward republican secularism rather than sectarian religion.

The dedication speech was just that, a speech not a sermon, delivered by respected Unitarian Joseph Story, who in 1811 at 32 had become the youngest Supreme Court Associate Justice. At Mt. Auburn's dedication, he spoke with judicious reason seasoned by personal emotion. He knew death's reality. A young daughter had recently died, the fifth child he lost in a span of fifteen years. To a sympathetic and understanding audience, Judge Story ably and eloquently summarized the cluster of Unitarian attitudes that converged in Mt. Auburn.

Story first spoke of the responsibility to the dead: "It is the duty of the living … to provide for the dead." But in the next sentence, he spoke of one's own mortal self-interest. "It is not a mere office of pious regard for others; but it comes home to our own bosoms, as those who are-soon to enter upon the common inheritance."

Story expanded on the mortal desire to be remembered: "We derive solace, nay, pleasure, from the reflection, that when the hour of separation comes, these earthly remains will still retain the tender regard of those; whom we leave behind;—that the spot, where they shall lie, will be remembered with a fond and soothing reverence;—that our children will visit it in the midst of their sorrows; and our kindred in remote generations feel that a local inspiration hovers round it."

Drawing on Old Testament references, Story proposed that we have an instinct for our earthly remains to repose in communion with our kindred and friends. He declared, "It is a matter of instinct, not of reasoning. It is a spiritual impulse, which supersedes belief, and disdains questions."

Story's remarks made it clear that Mt. Auburn served such fundamental, and even higher, human purposes: admonition, instruction, consolation, and more. "They admonish us, by their very silence, of our own frail and transitory being. They instruct us in the true value of life, and in its noble purposes, its duties, and its destination. They spread around us, in the reminiscences of the past, sources of pleasing, though melancholy reflection." Somewhat rhetorically, Story wondered why such a communion with the dead "is not made to exert a more profound influence?"

He waxed eloquently about the influences that a rightly selected and properly arranged cemetery, such as Mt. Auburn, offers. "They may preach lessons, to which none may refuse to listen, and which all, that live, must hear. Truths may be there felt and taught in the silence of our own meditations, more persuasive, and more enduring, than ever flowed from human lips. The grave hath a voice of eloquence, nay, of superhuman eloquence, which speaks at once to the thoughtlessness of the rash, and the devotion of the good; which addresses all times, and all ages, and all sexes; which tells of wisdom to the wise, and of comfort to the afflicted; which warns us of our follies and our dangers; which whispers to us in accents of peace, and alarms us in tones of terror; which steals with a healing balm into the stricken heart, and lifts up and supports the broken spirit; which awakens a new enthusiasm for virtue, and disciplines us for its severer trials and duties; which calls up the images of the illustrious dead, with an animating presence for our example and glory; and which demands of us, as men, as patriots, as christians, as immortals, that the powers given by God should be devoted to his service, and the minds created by his love, should return to him with larger capacities for virtuous enjoyment, and with more spiritual and intellectual brightness."

And of course, Story evoked the natural setting and the ministrations of Nature with its juxtaposition to the distant city. He mused that Mt. Auburn stood between two worlds, liminalities of the living and the dead, as well as of the country and the city. "We stand, as it were, upon the borders of two worlds; and as the mood of our minds may be, we may gather lessons of profound wisdom by contrasting the one with the other, or indulge in the dreams of hope and ambition, or solace our hearts by melancholy meditations." (Picturesque paintings of the day typically depicted rural ruins in the foreground with a village in the distance.)

Story began his final paragraph with an essential message, "Let us banish, then, the thought, that this is to be the abode of a gloom, which will haunt the imagination by its terrors, or chill the heart by its solitude."

Judge Story's dedicatory remarks for Mt. Auburn Cemetery summarized a Unitarian domestication of death framed by Nature. Death was rendered, somewhat paradoxically, more personal and less fearful. It fostered intimacies and awarenesses by evoking sensibilities and intuitions. Its agreeable melancholy honored yet limited grief, particularly for men who could then continue worldly pursuits. Death was removed from the exclusive authority of the church and religion, becoming more naturalistic and secular. It looked not to Christian deathways but to universal practices from the ages and various cultures for inspiration.

Such a Unitarian way became palpable in the garden cemeteries that followed Mt. Auburn's example. Twenty-four years after Story's dedicatory remarks at Mt. Auburn, Ralph Waldo Emerson offered dedicatory remarks for Sleepy Hollow Cemetery in Cambridge, where he and other famous Transcendentalists would be buried. He acknowledged how the making of garden cemeteries had spread: "Our people accepting this lesson from science, yet touched by the tenderness which Christianity breathes, have found a means in the consecration of gardens. A simultaneous movement has, in a hundred cities and towns in this country, selected some convenient piece of undulating ground with pleasant woods and waters; every family chooses its own clump of trees; and we lay the corpse in these leafy colonnades."

Throughout the nineteenth century, scores of garden cemeteries were created in American cities from Bangor, Maine to Kansas City, Missouri to New Orleans, Louisiana. The garden cemetery became a standard for interment and memoralization. This now familiar medium conveys a complex and persuasive message regarding death.

CREMATION: SANITATION AND PURIFICATION

The Civil War popularized embalming, preserving bodies at the battlefield so they could be shipped north and be afforded the standard funeral of the 19th century. Funerals of that era included the viewing of the body. Abraham Lincoln, assassinated on April 14, 1865, was embalmed and taken by train to his Springfield, Illinois home, reversing the route he had taken to Washington four years earlier. The funeral train travelled slowly with stops along the route from April 21 to May 3. Along the way, his body "lay in state" for public viewing. An estimated two hundred thousand filed past his remains. Such a display would not have been possible without embalming.

Arsenic was the original embalming agent, but was gradually displaced by formaldehyde, invented in 1867. New embalming technologies helped promote an emerging funeral industry complete with self-proclaimed professional morticians. Simultaneously, an alternative and controversial practice for disposal of bodies appeared with its own technology: cremation.

An efficient cremation chamber was displayed at the 1873 Vienna Exposition. The first American crematorium built in the southwestern Pennsylvania village of Washington, became the site of a widely publicized and controversial cremation in 1876. Anticipation of this first cremation had been building since 1874.

In that year, a spate of newspaper articles and two significant public addresses, one by a scientist and the second by a clergyman, brought cremation to a popular consciousness. The clergyman, Octavius B. Frothingham, had a quixotic Unitarian identity.

In his ministry, Frothingham had progressed from rational Christian Unitarianism, to Transcendentalism, and then to the Free Religious Association that generally opposed all institutional supernaturalisms. Frothingham served as the FRA's first president in 1867. In 1874, he was heading a New York City congregation, the Independent Liberal

Church. Frothingham represented the most radical element of nineteenth century Unitarianism.

In his 1876 sermon, "Disposal of Our Dead," preached before his New York City congregation, he proposed, "it is a subject that concerns us as human beings—not as adherents of a peculiar faith, or members of a particular church, or believers in a special creed. The movement in favor of cremation is not an infidel or pagan movement, but on in which a bishop may feel as deep an interest as a rationalist; a devotee as a doctor; a minister as a materialist; the most delicate and poetic, as the coarsest and most prosaic mind. Its significance is in its simple humanity."

Actually, cremation suited Frothingham's own antisupernatural and pro-scientific form of "free religion." His sermon revealed his essential bias.

The sermon began by demythologizing Christian burial practices as borrowed from the ancient Hebrews. Frothingham explained that the old Hebrews were scrupulous about burial, because they held to an idea: "the idea that the body contained, in some sense, the soul; and that its burial was somehow a guarantee of the soul's peace." Such a superstition, he elaborated, was something of a universal anxiety and yes, a superstition that had ties to belief in resurrection.

Elaborating on the popular notion of peace, that a body in the ground reposes peacefully, Frothingham vividly described the reality: "We know, on reflection, that this is illusion. We know that there is no stillness in the grave;

that Nature, which never rests, and allows no rest to organized or unorganized thing—Nature, which abhors rest, respecting not even the dread repose of death, seizes at once the cast-off body, and with occult chemistry and slow burning decomposes and consumes it. But the ancients did not know this as we do. That the body, left above ground, decayed, they perceived; and, to prevent the effect of it, would even resort to burning on occasion; but of all that went on beneath the ground they were not aware. They could not, therefore, be sensible, as we are, of the serious perils that were involved in their practice. That it endangered the health of the living they never conjectured."

Frothingham's ostensible reason for cremation involved sanitation—the public's health. But it was really a matter of his radical religious outlook that contended against all supernaturalisms. He gave himself away in arguing, "The common practice of interring the dead is positively pernicious to the living." But what caused the continuation of ground burial? Frothingham concluded that it was a matter of "old association." It is the duty of "true religion to desist from a custom which the old religions sanctioned. There are many who feel that it is a case of religion against religion; religion enlightened by knowledge and sweetened by humanity, against a religion clothed in an ignorance that could not be put off, and associated with rites that could not be dispensed." Cremation was an aspect of what Frothingham envisioned as a new, enlightened religion, a reformed religion that served the human common good.

Frothingham further argued that cremation through the rapid decomposition of fire "sublimated and purified" that which must die. The leading scholar of cremation Stephen Prothero titled his groundbreaking monograph on cremation "Purified by Fire." Frothingham was an early proponent of cremation's purifications, not only of the body but also of society's attitudes.

Beyond sanitation, there were other considerations he brought to bear: It is a relative inexpensive as well as quick way to dispose of the body. There is an aesthetic element: a pile of white ashes does not carry the terrifying sensations of the decomposing body. The ashes are portable; they can be carried away when residences are changed. But these were secondary considerations, relative to public sanitation and undermining traditional belief.

In conclusion, Frothingham gave definite shape to his ulterior motive. Frothingham used cremation as a wedge to sunder supernaturalism, first claiming that any religion or philosophy can incorporate cremation into its practices. "So far as any practice is founded on prejudice, and perpetuated as an outgrowth of theological belief, loyalty to our own rational conviction prompts us to suspect it, and, when in any way noxious, to assail and remove it. Each time this is done, ancient foundations are shaken. If it is done in a wise temper, friendly to truth and sympathetic with good, the old foundations will give place to new ones capable of sustaining a nobler structure. The practice of interment has been intimately associated with beliefs that we repudiate as superstitions."

Frothingham proved prophetic in predicting, "Nobody expects that such a change will be effected in a day. It must come gradually, and by slow degrees." By 2000, twenty-five percent of bodies in the United States were being cremated rather than interred. That percentage continues to grow.

A careful reading of Octavius B. Frothingham's pioneering sermon in favor of creation leaves no doubt that he challenged old traditions and their grounding superstitions to overturn supernatural theologies. Frothingham wanted to shake "ancient foundations."

From our vantage more than a century after Frothingham's cremation sermon, it appears he additionally anticipated the consumer's dilemma in disposing of body and understood the underlying psychology of the growing funeral industry's profits: "Avarice never looks so vile as when it would save a few miserable dollars by scrimping the decent arrangements of a funeral. It is only natural that we should lavish generously our tributes on the silent forms of those we have loved; that we should enclose them in precious wood, and cover them in seemly raiment, and make them fragrant with flowers. I would rather encourage this than rebuke it; and that it may be encouraged, I would reduce the unavoidable expense to the lowest practicable sum, thus allowing a margin for the pure gratification of feeling. The available means should not be quite exhausted in the bare task of putting the now useless form away from sight. Let the saddest and most indispensable part of the last rites tax no more, than cannot be avoided, the light purses of the artisan and mechanic; and let the most of what can be spared be put at the disposition of pure affection ; for this is consolation, while the other is agony. It is claimed already for cremation, and it will be claimed more and more, that it allows this margin, and thus plays into the hands of love."

MEMORIAL SOCIETY MOVEMENT

Throughout the next century, the funeral industry, led by a group of self-identified "professionals," known by various monikers, most prominently, *funeral director,* assumed various roles that ranged from undertaker/embalmer, to ritualist, to something like quasi-clergy. The funeral home increasingly became the place where death became culturally shrouded.

By the mid-twentieth century, the funeral industry had appropriated many death customs -- and reaped what was being judged obscene profits by psychologically and emotionally coercing the bereaved. Death was commercialized and the practitioners belonged to a self-promoting death industry.

Other factors played in the commercialization of death, including the influences of urbanization and mobility, which helped fragment communities and scatter families, the advancements of health care, the expansion of hospitals and long-term care facilities, and an increasing life span.

Increasingly in the twentieth century, the final years of aging and dying were being sequestered. Death was rendered invisible, out of sight and out of mind. And there was an efficient industry to dispose of bodies and to make and handle arrangements.

In response to this cold profit seeking commercialization of death, the Memorial Society Movement emerged. In 1939, the progressive Church of the People in Seattle under the leadership of Rev. Fred Shorter, organized the first memorial society, the People's Memorial Association (PMA), a non-profit concern. Shorter and his left- leaning congregation had a history of leftist cooperative ventures, run by and for the members.

That first memorial society endures and remembers the influences and impulses that led to its founding: "Prevailing funeral customs stressed embalming, display of the body and burial in a costly casket. The founders of PMA felt these practices ostentatious and emphasizing the material rather than spiritual aspects of death. They advocated for the choice of cremation and memorial services without the body present as a far more economical option. Their aim was to present a meaningful and beautiful service at a fraction of the cost."

Immediate cremation followed by a memorial service at a later convenient time and appropriate place set a precedent for the practices for subsequent, similar societies throughout the country. Eventually, other memorial societies, as did the PMA, allowed for other economical practices, including various aspects of the so-called traditional American funeral.

The author of this essay was once minister of the First Unitarian Church of Youngstown, Ohio, that had in the 1960s established its own memorial society. In a closet, unused for decades, was a theological red, brocade casket pall to be used to cover inexpensive "cardboard" caskets for in-church funeral services.

Memorial societies were not doctrinaire about the simple design they had started with: immediate cremation and later memorial service, but it was a standard that helped make more popular cremation first introduced to Americans in 1874. Among Unitarians, cremation became not only acceptable but popular.

Unitarian Ministers and their Churches took on the formation of local, non-profit memorial societies. (Jessica Mitford would remember that Unitarians, Quakers, intellectuals, and eggheads led the Memorial Society Movement.) The second memorial society, founded in New York City in 1947, had as a founder Unitarian minister Donald Harrington of the progressive Community Church. Rev. Robert Killam encouraged First Unitarian Church of Cleveland to organize in 1948 the Cleveland Memorial Society. The congregation continues to host the organization in its building. A pair of New Jersey Unitarian laity, Peter and Durinda Putnam, in 1954 initiated the Princeton Memorial Society, when there were only seven memorial societies in the nation.

The Cleveland and Princeton memorial societies provided a model for progressive and activist Unitarians to follow, according to those who founded the Philadelphia Memorial Society in 1956. A committee of First Unitarian Church of Philadelphia met and organized "a public, non-denominational agency similar to those in Cleveland and Princeton" using the words of those two organizations to establish their new Memorial Society of Greater Philadelphia.

Unitarians were significant participants in the Memorial Society Movement that began after World War II. Some two hundred non-profit memorial societies were eventually founded, and ninety of those survive.

While serving a Seattle Unitarian Church through 1949, Josiah Bartlett became familiar with the memorial society movement through the groundbreaking People's Memorial Association. While living in the San Francisco area, in 1957 he and his wife Laile helped found the Bay Area Memorial Society in their living room, as he later noted, "in front of a fireplace."

When the Bartletts hosted the exploratory meeting to form a San Francisco area memorial society in 1957, they were likely playing a hand in the book Jessica Mitford would write six years later. Bartlett later remembered, "At the meeting was Robert Truehaft, the lawyer husband of Jessica Mitford who, some years afterwards, wrote *The American Way of Death*, which became a best seller."

The Memorial Society Movement anticipated the consumer protest against the funeral industry that muckraker journalist Jessica Mitford ignited in 1963 with *The American Way of Death*, arguably one of the significant books of the second half of the twentieth century.

Mitford, as a journalist, articulated a funeral reform movement that already had captured the public's imagination. A 1961 *Saturday Evening Post* article measured the public's disgust with the funeral industry of 1961. Mitford was featured in the article, as was Unitarian Minister Josiah Bartlett. He expressed a Unitarian sensibility about the commercialization of death. "My people are in increasing rebellion against the pagan atmosphere of the modern funeral. It is not so much the cost as the morbid sensibility of dwelling on the physical remains…. [The funeral societies] vowed to work together for simpler and more dignified funerals which are not a vain and wasteful expense and do not emphasize the mortal and material remains rather than the triumph of the human spirit."

LIFE'S FINAL RITE: A CELEBRATION

Josiah Bartlett's implication that Unitarians of mid twentieth century emphasized "the triumph of the human spirit" had already resulted in new funeral and memorial service liturgies that had several significant elements. The eulogy was the focus, meaning an intimate appraisal of the deceased from information gathered from family, friends, and acquaintances. Around the eulogy, readings and remarks addressed the needs of those gathered in a special community of grief and remembrance. Good music, often of a secular nature, was important when possible. Those who wished to speak from the congregation were encouraged to offer personal anecdotes and remembrances. Though an informal liturgy, compared to scripts that had prevailed in denominational hymnals, ministers who practiced the art of the last rite of passage in this reformed way sought beauty of word and design, as well as exploration of the meanings of the occasion.

There wasn't one rite, rather a general way and an appropriate flow from beginning to end, building to the eulogy. Informally, readings of poetry and prose circulated among the clergy. Each minister had a cache of varied literary choices to suit varied circumstances. A primary resource was a Beacon Press anthology from 1929 gathered by Unitarian minister Robert French Leavens.

The collection, *Great Companions*, included a section "Intimations of Immortality."

One of the best practitioners of the evolving art of the funeral, Rev. Robert Terry Weston, produced a collection of selections that included many of his own writings. *Cup of Strength: Readings in Time of Sorrow and Bereavement*, published as a 69-page book by his Lexington, MA Unitarian congregation in 1945, became an underground classic for Unitarian ministers. (Rev. Paul Beattie, of All Souls Unitarian Church, Indianapolis IN issued a mimeographed copy in 1972.)

Weston's "Foreword" counseled, "The minister will find it more useful if he will freely alter and combine elements to make whatever combinations and applications as may seem appropriate to each case. In ministering to grief, the primary obligation is not the fidelity of authorship, but that of meeting an immediate need for help or comfort." He further counseled, "Remembering this, the minister ought therefore to hold firmly in mind that a time of bereavement is not a time for theological argument. Comfort must be given as nearly a possible within the patterns of the minister's own beliefs. It is hoped that this collection may offer help to those who can no longer subscribe to the traditional beliefs."

Weston had the humanistic worldview that came to characterize much of non-creedal, twentieth century Unitarianism. Among Unitarian and Universalist ministers religious humanism ranged from naturalistic mysticism to an ethical religion nearly secular. Weston's own writing, though rational and at times scientific, was marbled with reverence and mysticism, in language that was like free verse poetry. Here's a typical passage from his 1945 collection: "Out of the mystery of life we have come, and into it we return. In mystery our whole life is lived, nor may any man see beyond the veil of physical existence. Yet in the little knowledge we do taste, there is a suggestion of a mystery more sublime and wonderful than life."

In the fruitful decade following the 1961 merger of the Universalists and Unitarian, Universalist minister and writer, Carl Seaburg, published through Beacon Press an important anthology, *Great Occasions: Readings for the Celebration of Birth, Coming-of-Age, Marriage, and Death*, 1968. (The current Unitarian Universalist Association's publishing house, Skinner House Books, republished the original Beacon Press hardcover edition in paperback in 2001.) Similar to Weston, Seaburg had a special focus for the non- traditional end of life service, by this era often being called "celebration of life." Seaburg acknowledged the increase of the non-church affiliated in the culture, the disintegration of old theologies, and the influence of memorial societies on traditional funerals as factors begging for new liturgical ways.

Great Occasions remains a standard. In it, Seaburg built on the Unitarian and now Unitarian Universalist point of view regarding death. In his introduction to "Death," he wrote, "[F]unreal and memorial services fulfill a social need as well as an individual one. They provide…for a dignified disposal of the body, aid the bereaved to reorient themselves, and while publicly acknowledging and commemorating the dead person, reassert the viability of the group."

Moreover, Seaburg explained: "The funeral or memorial service…is a chance to restate the relationships between a man and what the values, and between a man and his fellows. In essence, we say that is good to have lived, that death fits into life and helps it make what little sense it does, and that all remains well with Life and the universe. It is not the place of an empty eulogy of the departed. Many of today's clergy are showing great skill in their ability to blend honest personal comments into an artistic whole." Seaburg provided 451 readings to put mortality and death into context. For generations of Unitarian Universalist clergy, Seaburg's anthology was the primary resource when fashioning funerals and memorial services.

In 1993, Skinner House Books published this author's *In Memoriam: Modern Funeral and Memorial Services*. A second edition was released in 2000. While intended to be a clergy resource, another audience was the laity, who might then be enabled to lead a memorial service or even funeral by using one of the varied scripts as is or with editing and adding materials.

In Memoriam also added practical advice for the necessary arrangements, making a distinction between a funeral (immediate with body present) and memorial service (usually with cremation and at a later date). In part, information and counsel sought to empower those entrusted with dealing with a death in their dealings with an end of life provider. This informed consumer intention was secondary to the service.

A few of the book's service scripts reflected the author's natural religion/humanistic orientation that had once solidly characterized post-merger Unitarian Universalism. There was an explicit theistic service. In addition, a Quaker-inspired silent service, ceremonies using flowers and quilt squares, and a service of candles offered unique ritual and innovation. With such innovation, the author reflected contemporary trends that had transformed Unitarian Universalism: feminism; earth-centered religions, including neo-paganism and Native American practices; a renewed interest in theistic spirituality. An interment (graveside) service explicated the taking of death out into Nature, remembering the intentions of the garden cemetery movement, while offering tangible closure to the first days of loss and grief.

The author fashioned each specimen service with a eulogy at its heart. Above all else, no matter the shape of the service, the deceased's life needs to be portrayed lovingly and realistically, artfully drawing out the essences, as well as life-affirming particulars, blending the personal with the universal. How to go about writing a eulogy by consulting family and friends was described.

The author's specimen services incorporated an increasing wisdom around the grief process, made popular by 1969 *On Death and Dying* by Elisabeth Kübler-Ross. Her five stages of grief provided a template for good grieving. Earlier Unitarian ministers intuited what Kübler-Ross codified.

As the first years of a new century and millennium progressed, on behalf of Skinner House Books the author took on the honored task of editing a new collection of readings for the four great rites of passage, similar to *Great Occasions*. The project resulted in four separate collections. *Beyond Absence: A Treasury of poems, Quotations and readings on Death and Remembrance* continued the Unitarian and Unitarian Universalist accumulation of inspiring and useful material for dealing death. Robert Terry Weston's 1945 collection, *A Cup of Strength*, while intended to be a clergy resource, the reading were appropriate for personal reflection on mortality by a general audience. *Beyond Absence* was also a resource intended to serve clergy and a larger humanity.

The readings in *Beyond Absence* intentionally drew on contemporary Unitarian Universalist clergy, especially seeking out the voices of women.

In addressing the reader, the author wrote, "Throughout the ages, human beings have been understandably ambivalent about death, perhaps never more so than now. In many parts of the world, we sequester those who are elderly or ill. No longer is the body washed at home or laid out in the living room for viewing. We hand over the physical details of death to specialists. When death comes, we may be repulsed, fearful, or simply unprepared. These readings offer a blessed intimacy with an inevitable and defining aspect of the human condition.

"I chose these words with an eye towards the insight of bereavement counseling, which respects the complex and conflicted impact death might have on the dying and the ripple effect death has on survivors.

"This project …involves nothing less than the meaning of the human condition."

DEATH AND DYING AMONG CONTEMPORARY UNITARIAN UNIVERSALISTS

Unitarians had an abiding interest in reforming American deathways. They significantly influenced, intellectually and practically, how the greater culture deals with the overarching reality of the human condition: mortality and death. Unitarian innovations and reforms cited in this essay served to domesticate death in the name of the universal human condition; challenged traditions and the supernaturalisms that supported those traditions; resisted the commercialization of death by a funeral industry; and lifted up the dignity and worth of the deceased through artful and meaningful "celebrations of life."

There is a palpable Unitarian Universalist way for meeting death, though that way is not prescribed. Remember, Unitarian Universalism is non-creedal, as well as progressive. Its ethos has continually encouraged the proving of all things while holding on to that which is good. This search for truth has been tempered, humanized, by love. To seek the truth in love is an enduring mantra. That notion of love has many dimensions, ranging from love of self and others like one's self to a love of Life and its often-inscrutable ways.

Here are markers of Unitarian Universalism's contemporary, convergent attitudes and understandings regarding death.

Death should not be invisible. Death is a hard reality both to accept within one's own mortality and to experience through a beloved. The American culture has devised strategies of denial. Yet death is a pathway to living fully, even joyfully, in the moment. The ancient philosophers, the Stoics in particular, counseled *memento mori* to be regularly reminded that living is dying, not obsessively, but now and again to give living context and perspective.

Think of Unitarian Universalist ways in terms of the **domestication of death**, coming to a certain intimacy with death through a variety of attitudes, behaviors, and strategies: *memento mori*, including contemplation of mortality in a garden cemetery or similar setting, not sequestering the aged or dying, leaving the body in a natural (unembalmed) state, tangibly commemorating the deceased, and through subsequent years remembering.

Death should be conditioned by Nature. This might be literal, that is, interring the body, or cremation remains in a garden cemetery or similar natural setting. Cremation allows many options, including scattering at a meaningful site or several sites. Unitarian Universalist churches may have a carefully designed cremation garden or more informally include the ashes in a planting, the tree or shrub serving as a living memorial. Furthermore, **death should be construed as part and parcel of Nature's cycles of Life continuing through the generations—a natural phenomenon**. Being natural, death is right and fitting in Nature's scheme. Nature inspires a richer living through acceptance of mortality's place in the Web of Life.

Death of a loved one, friend, or member of a community should be observed in an artfully crafted funeral or memorial service. In this service, a formal eulogy or a series of individual remembrances speak with loving truth of the life that the deceased chose to live, the influences that played on her or him through the years, how she or he shaped our common world, and what of that person endures in us. With a dignified service and the promise to remember, the deceased have has a blessed assurance that in death and repose there might be a peace said to pass understanding.

Unitarian Universalist ministers should be, and generally are, well prepared to plan and conduct funeral and memorial services, entrusted by their congregations and a larger community to navigate the complexities of end of life concerns and rituals. This includes grief-counseling skills. A Unitarian Universalist minister seeks to express **transcendent meanings**, such as the continuing influence of love that the deceased brought into the world—a love that endures and is passed on through the generations.

The funeral and memorial service should address the varied grief that the family and gathered community are experiencing. This includes a continuing promise to remain steadfast for those who grieve, acknowledging that grief is an extended process, unique to each person who grieves.

Death should be planned for. This planning has certain aspects. Every individual should leave instructions about final wishes. This includes the practical and existential, what is often included in a Living Will, regarding the parameters of medical procedures to take or not to take in one's final days. A Living Will often designates a trusted person to have Power of Attorney for Health Care, charged to make ultimate decisions. Such a directive often is accompanied by a designation of the same or other person to have a fiscal Power of Attorney. Of course, a legally drawn will alleviates hindrances and complications of the deceased's estate. Valuable, too, are instructions regarding final rites; this includes disposition of the body, burial or scattering. Instructions might include memorialization, such as cemetery plot and monument, but also designated charities for contributions in the deceased's memory. **It is good to memorialize in tangible forms**; and for those who survive, it is good to visit memorials, respecting and remembering. Also important are directives for the funeral or memorial service: music, readings, participants, officiant, location, and the like, again in consultation with family and clergy.

It is good to **do such planning in conversation with family and perhaps clergy.** This models how to confront death, honestly and compassionately, letting genuine feeling have its full day. Such planning has benefits when death comes with grief in its wake.

Such planning addresses considerations around **consumer concerns regarding funeral providers**. A valuable resource is the not-for-profit Funeral Consumers Alliance (FCA) successor to the memorial society movement's national organization. The FCA declares, "We are the only 501(c) (3) nonprofit organization dedicated to protecting a consumer's right to choose a meaningful, dignified, affordable funeral. We offer education and advocacy to consumers nationwide and are not affiliated with the funeral industry." The FCA website has many valuable resources to inform and guide.

Typically, after a house and car, a funeral is a person's third greatest life expenditure. End of life arrangements should not be undertaken during duress, when circumstances are pressing and emotions are vulnerable to compliance techniques. All involved should counsel together about desired arrangements before death comes.

Hospice care, often at home, has become an increasing choice for Unitarian Universalists. This fits earlier considerations regarding the domestication of death.

An emerging option among Unitarian Universalists is **green burial**, allowing the unembalmed body, often in a simple shroud, to decompose naturally in a natural setting. This reflects scruples about cremation's effects on the environment, particularly the energy required to fire the crematorium. Green burial also looks to the body's constituent parts leaching back into Nature. (In advocating for a rural cemetery in the early nineteenth century, Unitarians cited a dramatic example of Nature's embrace of the body. When the body of Major John Andre was exhumed in 1821, his skull was held and pierced by roots of a peach tree. For those advocates of the taking death into the countryside, this offered a romantic and compelling example of "Nature's embrace.") Today, green burial resonates to the Unitarian Universalist seventh principle: "respect for the interdependent web of existence of which we are all a part."

There is no doubt that the first principle of Unitarian Universalism (1985), "the inherent worth and dignity of every person," summarizes, as well informs this liberal religion's attitudes regarding its deathways. Through two centuries, Unitarian Universalists have increasingly emphasized the personal and universally human, especially above traditional dogma and theology.

Unitarian Universalist reforms and innovations around death and dying emphasize essential human dignity. Unitarian Universalists find the human condition transcendent and sacred.

As the author intoned in *In Memoriam:*

A human life is sacred.
It is sacred in its being born.
It is sacred in its living.
And it is sacred in its dying.

Made in the USA
Thornton, CO
05/27/22 07:23:56

f27a7ea4-15ab-4049-9556-35786228345cR01